INNER
STRUGGLES

John Phillips

Copyright © John Phillips

First Edition
Published in 2015 by BeaconLight Trust,
150 High Street, Banstead,
Surrey, SM7 2NZ,
United Kingdom

Email: books@beaconlight.co.uk

ISBN 978-1-906526-12-2

Design: Mel Dixey
Cover Design: Lucy Jacques
Printed by Printbridge,
16 Castle Street, Bodmin,
Cornwall, PL31 2DU

Acknowledgements

One of the things I collect is ideas. Most of them remain ideas. This little book is the evidence that occasionally – very occasionally – I manage to do something with an idea.

Many people have helped me and many more have encouraged me over the past few months. I am very grateful to every one of them.

I must thank Barbara Parsons. All who read this book will benefit from her special gift with words: her gift has been well used to refine my own efforts.

Mel Dixey has been responsible for the design, with Lucy Jacques designing the cover. They are both very creative and I am extremely fortunate, and grateful, that they were willing to work with me – with such an excellent result.

I am thankful to Nicola Goddard who undertook the proof-reading. I would never contemplate going to print with anything until the proof had passed through Nicola's hands – and under her eyes!

Finally, I am especially grateful to Dr Paul Adams, Executive Chair of BeaconLight Trust, who has shown remarkable patience in supporting me with many hours of his time. His wisdom has been of immense value.

John Phillips
May 2015

Contents

Introduction

Life is a mixture of happiness and pain; of laughter and tears; of celebration and grief; of soaring and crawling. For some, life brings more joy than sorrow; for others, life is hard with only rare moments of real joy. For us all, there are times when we struggle.

Sadly, our personal struggles can be the result of our own mistakes and unwise choices but, often, they result from circumstances which we have not caused and which we cannot control. Whatever the cause of your own struggles, I hope that you will find comfort and help in this little book.

If you have a personal faith in Jesus Christ, the book will encourage you to keep your focus on Him and on the truth of the Bible. You must always remember that you are never alone as you struggle.

If you are unfamiliar with the Christian faith, I trust that this book will cause you to look to Jesus. He is able to meet your deepest needs. I trust, too, that the book will encourage you to explore what it means to have a personal relationship with Him. God longs that every one of us might know Him personally as His child, as we journey through both the joyful and the sad seasons of life.

I pray that this little book will bring you hope and faith and comfort in God. I am confident that it will, as the focus is on His words, taken from the Bible, and not on mine.

John Phillips

INNER STRUGGLES

ABANDONED?

In the Psalms we read:

> **Those who know your name trust in you, for you, O LORD, do not abandon those who search for you.**
> Psalm 9:10 (NLT)

> **Even if my father and mother abandon me, the LORD will hold me close.**
> Psalm 27:10 (NLT)

To be abandoned by a partner or long-term friend, or even your parents, must be truly devastating. We often take it for granted that those whom we have trusted over many years will always stick by us.

Jesus knows what it means to be abandoned. He was abandoned by His closest disciples, hours before His arrest and trial. The Bible tells us that Jesus' soul was overwhelmed with sorrow. Twice He discovered His disciples asleep, after He had asked them to keep watch while He spent time alone to pray.

The following day, one of those disciples, Peter, repeatedly denied that he knew Jesus, just as Jesus said he would. At the time when Jesus most needed their support, the disciples abandoned Him.

Unlike His disciples and unlike anyone else, Jesus will always remain faithful to everyone who seeks Him and chooses to follow Him. He will never abandon them. No one could want a better friend, not only for this life but for ever.

DEAR FATHER GOD

I feel as though I have been abandoned and I need someone who, I can be sure, will always be there for me. Please help me to understand how I can know Jesus.

AMEN

ANGRY?

The Apostle Paul wrote:

> **'In your anger do not sin': do not let the sun go down while you are still angry...**
>
> Ephesians 4:26

Anger is a very powerful emotion and we all get angry. At times it is right to be angry.

It is right to be angry at the widespread injustice within our society. And it is right to show anger when, for example, the most vulnerable people, especially children and the elderly, are abused.

The Apostle Paul gives us two instructions. Firstly, he warns us against failing to control our anger. When not controlled, it can so easily cause us to act unwisely, perhaps by taking revenge against a person.

Secondly, Paul tells us not to hold on to anger, for it can quickly lead to deep-seated resentment and bitterness, which can linger for weeks, months and even years. When that happens, we inflict so much pain upon ourselves.

If there is someone with whom you are angry (or perhaps the anger has already turned to bitterness), why not ask God to help you to forgive the person? Why not put the anger or bitterness behind you?

DEAR FATHER GOD

I realise that my anger has become such a part of my life and I do not want it any longer. Please help me to put this incident behind me - forever. Please help me to forgive (*the person's name*).

AMEN

ANXIOUS?

The Apostle Paul wrote:

Do not be anxious about anything, but in every situation, by prayer and petition, with thanksgiving, present your requests to God. And the peace of God, which transcends all understanding, will guard your hearts and your minds in Christ Jesus.

Philippians 4:6-7

Nothing can bring greater joy than knowing Jesus. For this reason, Paul has just told the Christians in Philippi that they should always rejoice.

But he realises that there is one thing, above all else, which can rob them of their joy – anxiety. Those who have never suffered from it, other than the usual nervousness associated with such events as exams (and awaiting the results!), will not realise how destructive anxiety can be.

Paul's instruction is very clear. Whatever the circumstances or the reasons for the anxiety, they should not keep it to themselves (or even just share it with others). They should speak to God about it, asking for His help.

There is no promise that the cause of the anxiety will be immediately resolved. However, they can expect God to protect their hearts and minds with His peace.

When anxiety comes, what do you do? Do you keep it to yourself, perhaps until it becomes too unbearable? Paul's advice is the much better option.

DEAR FATHER GOD

I do get anxious over all sorts of issues. Even now, I am anxious about (*explain the anxiety*). Please show me how I should try to deal with this. And please guard my heart and mind with your peace.

AMEN

ASHAMED?

The Apostle Paul wrote:

… if you declare with your mouth, 'Jesus is Lord,' and believe in your heart that God raised him from the dead, you will be saved.

As Scripture says, 'Anyone who believes in him will never be put to shame.'

Romans 10:9,11

Jesus encountered two women who had reason to be ashamed. One was a Samaritan whom Jesus met as she was drawing water at a well. Jesus knew that she had had five husbands and was now living with another man.[1]

Jesus met the other woman when she intruded on a dinner party at which He was a guest. She was well known as a woman of 'ill-repute'. As she anointed Jesus' feet with an expensive perfume, she wept: no doubt, her tears were tears of shame.[2]

Jesus did not condemn them. He spoke to them with gentleness and kindness. And they responded to Him, knowing that they had been forgiven and could put their shame behind them.

If you are struggling with shame, whether you have managed to hide it from others or whether it is 'in the open', why not bring it to Jesus? He already knows about it and is ready to receive you and forgive you.

DEAR FATHER GOD

I have done things of which I am ashamed, especially (*name the things which are causing the shame*). I realise that they have never been hidden from You. Please forgive me and please release me from my shame.

AMEN

[1]John 4:7-26; [2]Luke 7:36-50

CONDEMNED?

The Apostle Paul wrote:

> Therefore, there is now no condemnation
> for those who are in Christ Jesus...
>
> Romans 8:1

King David wrote:

> The LORD will rescue his servants;
> no one who takes refuge in him
> will be condemned.
>
> Psalm 34:22

The world is eager to condemn but God is eager to forgive. And it is God's forgiveness that really counts.

God can only forgive those who are 'in Christ Jesus'. He will forgive them for all the wrong they have done. He will do so because Jesus Himself has taken the punishment which we deserve. Jesus did that when He was condemned to death in place of us.

That is why God does not condemn us if we are 'in Christ Jesus': Jesus has already paid the price for our sins.

Try not to worry about other people judging you and condemning you. It may be painful but it will not last forever. However, if God condemns you, His punishment will last forever - for eternity.

We all have a decision to make: to face God's condemnation or to receive His forgiveness. If you have never asked God to forgive you, will you do so now? What is involved is fully explained on pages 90-97.

DEAR FATHER GOD

I understand the choice I have to make; to be with Jesus or to be outside of Jesus; to be forgiven or to stand condemned. I choose Jesus and your forgiveness. Please forgive me.

AMEN

CRUSHED?

King David wrote:

**The righteous cry out, and the LORD hears them;
he delivers them from all their troubles.
The LORD is close to the broken-hearted
and saves those who are crushed in spirit.**

Psalm 34:17-18

David wrote many Psalms in order to pour out his deepest feelings to God. There were times when he was compelled to pour out his thanks and praise to Him for all His goodness.

At other times he was in a really difficult situation and could see no way out: he felt crushed by his circumstances. Yet, even in those very dark times, he knew that God had not deserted him.

Jesus Himself chose to engage with those who most needed Him: those whom society looked to crush. It was not that others did not need Jesus: they were just too blind to see their need. The religious leaders were especially critical of Jesus. They taunted Him as being a 'friend of sinners'.

No one, whatever their status in society, could ask for a better friend than Jesus, the Son of God. If you feel crushed or broken, turn to God. Allow Him to come alongside you and restore you.

DEAR FATHER GOD

I do feel crushed and I cannot see any way out of my situation. I have tried just about everything and I have now run out of ideas. God, I do need Your help. Will You please restore me?

AMEN

DESPAIRING?

The Apostle Paul wrote:

> We are hard pressed on every side, but not crushed; perplexed, but not in despair;

2 Corinthians 4:8

> May the God of hope fill you with all joy and peace as you trust in him, so that you may overflow with hope by the power of the Holy Spirit.

Romans 15:13

When we are on the brink of despairing, it is natural to want to cling on to the hope that there might be 'light at the end of the tunnel'. But if we cannot see the end of the tunnel, our hope can so easily begin to slip away.

As we lose hope, despair can take its place. We may begin to imagine the worst possible outcomes to the situation which we are facing. That can be exceptionally draining – and painful.

The Apostle Paul suffered incredibly: at various times he was whipped, stoned and imprisoned. And yet, he did not reach the point of despairing. He had no reason to despair because he trusted 'the God of hope'.

For Paul, hope did not simply mean wishful thinking; rather, it was an absolute confidence that God would not fail him. Today, Christians have that same hope, a hope which will never give way to despair.

DEAR FATHER GOD

I know that I am losing hope. I cannot face the prospect of being in utter despair. Please help me to put my trust in You, so that my hope is restored and that You will help me.

AMEN

Jason's*
Story

> I pulled off the road and 'phoned one of my partners at the surgery. "I'm afraid I've broken down", I managed to blurt out. "Oh, that's OK we'll get the RAC out to you," cheerily replied my bemused colleague. I explained that the RAC would be of no help: I had had the breakdown, not the car!

Taking on too many tasks, whilst not giving sufficient time to my family, had led to a constant sense of being driven and out of control. With hindsight, coming to a sudden halt was a good thing.

It was a frightening time for us as a family. And there were to be dark times ahead. Counselling - and medication - was needed to restore me to health.

... I had a deep sense of God's presence and of His care.

Alongside that, my faith was so crucial. It is when we experience tough struggles that our faith is really tested. It is only then that we know whether God does actually fulfil the promises He has made in the Bible. And I can testify that He does. He certainly sustained me over the period of my illness: I had a deep sense of His presence and of His care.

It was also a time when God showed me things which I needed to change. In particular, two Scripture verses have remained with me from that time:

- "… he (*Jesus*) said to them (*his disciples*), 'Come with me by yourselves to a quiet place and get some rest.'"[1]

- "… And those who walk in pride he is able to humble.'"[2]

These verses reminded me, firstly, that we must pace our lives and take time out to rest and, secondly, that I had become far too confident in my own capability and less dependent on God.

I am very thankful that I did not have to go through that dark period of my life without God to hold me, even carry me.

[1]Mark 6:31; [2]Daniel 4:37b
*Not the real name of this person

DISCOURAGED?

God's words to Joshua:

> '...Have I not commanded you? Be strong and courageous. Do not be afraid; do not be discouraged, for the LORD your God will be with you wherever you go.'
>
> Joshua 1:9

Discouragement has been spoken of as a disease. If we think of it in that way, then it must be the most common of all diseases! We have all suffered from it and we will always be at risk of being 'infected' again: a discouraged person can quickly discourage others!

We can become discouraged when we fail to achieve our objectives and plans (or if we fear that we might fail) or if we meet unexpected obstacles. We can also become discouraged by criticism.

After Moses had died, God knew the enormous responsibility which Joshua would be taking on as leader of the Israelites. He encouraged Joshua with the promise that He would always be with him. With that promise, Joshua could be strong and courageous and not be afraid or get discouraged.

If you are facing discouragement, why not ask God to help you to be strong and courageous? If you are trusting in Him, then that promise to Joshua is for you also.

DEAR FATHER GOD

You know how easily discouraged I get because of the difficulties I am facing and the criticism I am getting. Thank You for always being with me. Please take away my fear, help me to be strong and give me the courage I need to move forward.

AMEN

DISTRESSED?

Words of Jesus:

> He took Peter, James and John along with him, and he began to be deeply distressed and troubled. 'My soul is overwhelmed with sorrow to the point of death,' he said to them. 'Stay here and keep watch.'
>
> Mark 14:33-34

We must never think that, because Jesus was God, He was immune from suffering and trouble when He lived on earth. He was both God and Man and He experienced all the emotions that we experience.

Therefore, it was right that He was deeply distressed shortly before He was to be arrested. He cried out to his Father, 'Please take this cup of suffering away from me. Yet I want your will to be done, not mine.'[1] Jesus knew the horrendous suffering which the crucifixion would bring but He was willing to obey God's wishes.

Jesus provides that supreme example for us to follow when we are distressed. Often, the only thing we can do is pray. It is always the best thing.

Are you in deep distress over something? If you have not yet prayed, do so now. Your prayer will be heard by Jesus Himself, now at God's right hand. He knows exactly how you are feeling.

DEAR FATHER GOD

It is comforting to know that You understand exactly how distressed I am. Everything is possible for You. Please (*make your personal request*). Please help me to accept whatever is Your will and give me the strength I need.

AMEN

[1]Mark 14:36 (NLT)

EMPTY?

The Apostle Peter wrote:

> **For you know that God paid a ransom
> to save you from the empty life
> you inherited from your ancestors.
> And it was not paid with mere
> gold or silver, which lose their value.
> It was the precious blood of Christ,
> the sinless, spotless Lamb of God.**
>
> 1 Peter 1:18-19 (NLT)

Even people with busy lives may complain that their life is empty. Despite being so busy – and perhaps too busy – they recognise that something is missing: they are not being fulfilled.

Although wealthy and powerful, it would seem that King Solomon, the son of King David, experienced that sense of emptiness. He was renowned for his great wisdom and he concluded that life is "meaningless, a chasing after the wind."[1]

About 1,000 years later the Apostle Peter wrote of the Christians' empty way of life before they put their trust in Jesus. And Jesus Himself said that He had come in order that people might have life to the full.[2]

If you feel your life is empty of meaning, do not try to fill it with pleasures or possessions. They will fail to satisfy you. Instead, look to Jesus. Only He can meet your deepest needs. Only He can bring real meaning to your life - a life that is full and satisfying.

DEAR FATHER GOD

I know my life is empty of meaning and purpose. If Jesus came to earth to give people life that is truly satisfying, then I need to understand what it means to have Jesus in my life. Please help me.

AMEN

[1]Ecclesiastes 2:17; [2]John 10:10

ENSLAVED?

Words of Jesus:

> Jesus replied, 'Very truly I tell you,
> everyone who sins is a slave to sin.
> Now a slave has no permanent place
> in the family, but a son belongs to it
> for ever. So if the Son sets you free,
> you will be free indeed...'

John 8:34-36

Almost 30 million people are thought to be living as slaves across the world today. That is a truly astonishing figure. But should we be so horrified that men and women will control and use and abuse fellow human beings?

The slave 'owners' are themselves slaves, for the Bible tells us that we are all slaves to sin (that is, we rebel against God), unless Jesus has set us free.

When Jesus does set us free, we are 'born again' with a new nature. And with our new nature comes a new desire; a desire to live to please God as we take our place in His family. We will not be perfect and will continue to sin. But we will no longer be controlled by that old sinful nature which enslaves us.

Have you yet been released from your life of slavery? If not, are you ready to begin a new life of true freedom, as a child of God? How you can do that - and what it means to be 'born again' - is explained on pages 90-97.

DEAR FATHER GOD

I know that I am a slave to sin. I do not seem to be in control of my own life. I feel as though someone else is controlling me. I do things I really do not want to do. Jesus, please set me free.

AMEN

Rod's Story

"Unlike many who end up in prison, I cannot blame my life of drugs, gambling and crime on my parents. They are Christians and I could not have asked for a better childhood. But I rejected God when I was 17.

I am just grateful that my parents never rejected me. It was a book which my mum sent to me in prison which, eventually, proved to be a turning point.

The book, *Run, Baby, Run,* was the story of Nicky Cruz, a notorious gang leader who became a Christian at a meeting in New York, having gone there in order to 'do over' the preacher.

But that night, Nicky heard that God was not interested in his past – whatever he had done - but only in his future.

'Could God forgive me for all of this?'

As I read, I reflected on my own life – the drugs, the crime, all the lying and betrayals, and the hurt and devastation I had caused my family. I asked myself, 'Could God forgive me for all of this?'

Tears began to pour down my face as I read that Nicky Cruz gave his life to God that night and as I thought about my situation.

Within a matter of weeks, I knew the answer to my own question, 'Yes, God was willing to forgive me and He longed to do so.' I received His forgiveness as I accepted Jesus into my life.   I was now free – even in prison.

'Yes, God was willing to forgive me and He longed to do so.'

And from Rod's mum:

> 'Finding out that your son or daughter is a drug addict and a criminal must be one of the most heart-wrenching things you can experience.
>
> 'But eventually there came a day of joy years later. In a letter, Rod told me that he had become a Christian and now knew that God was real. My heart was filled with joy and I couldn't stop thanking God for answering my prayers!
>
> 'One thing I have learned is to never give up hope. There is always hope.'

You can read Rod's story in 'The Real Deal' by Rod Williams www.therealdeal.org.uk

GRIEVING?

Words of King David:

> The LORD is my shepherd, I lack nothing.
> He makes me lie down in green pastures,
> he leads me beside quiet waters...
>
> Even though I walk through the
> darkest valley, I will fear no evil,
> for you are with me;
> your rod and your staff,
> they comfort me.

Psalm 23:1-2,4

We can all expect to experience grief at some point in our lives, notably through death but perhaps also through divorce or separation.

As we grieve, we need someone to journey with us; someone willing to spend time with us but only when we need them; someone willing to talk with us but only when we wish to talk; someone willing to listen when we do not want advice;

someone willing to cry with us; someone willing to accept our outbursts of anger.

There is no better person to journey with through the darkest valleys than Jesus. He always knows our deepest thoughts and our deepest needs. He will never leave those who choose to journey with Him, either through the valleys or over the hills.

It is good to have family members and close friends who will walk with you as you grieve but accept Jesus as that very best friend. You can depend upon Him totally.

DEAR FATHER GOD

I am thankful for the friends who are trying to help me but they do not really understand how I am feeling. And they don't know what to say. But You must understand completely. Please comfort me and help me through my grief.

AMEN

GUILT-RIDDEN?

Words of the Apostle:

> How much more, then, will the blood of
> Christ, who through the eternal Spirit offered
> himself unblemished to God, cleanse our
> consciences from acts that lead to death,
> so that we may serve the living God!
>
> Hebrews 9:14

> Let us draw near to God with a sincere heart
> and with the full assurance that faith brings,
> having our hearts sprinkled to cleanse us
> from a guilty conscience ...
>
> Hebrews 10:22

In a shop recently, I was overwhelmed by the range of cleaning products, with special products for each type of surface and each type of stain. I was delighted when I spotted a multi-purpose cleaner!

Stains spoil the appearance of the fabric (or carpet or surface) and it is very satisfying when you find the right product to remove them.

The worst stains are not to be found in our home but within us. They are the stains of our guilt. They are the result of the things which we have done and now regret. The very worst stains can be very difficult to live with.

There is just one remedy for our stains; the blood of the Lord Jesus Christ. Jesus had never sinned Himself and was the perfect sacrifice, offered to God in our place. To receive God's forgiveness – and have our guilty conscience cleansed – we must turn to Jesus Christ.

DEAR FATHER GOD

The guilt I am carrying around with me is just too much. How can I get rid of it? I keep asking myself why I did those things. Will You please help me? I do not believe anyone else can.

AMEN

HUNGRY?

Words of Jesus:

> Then Jesus declared, 'I am the bread of
> life. Whoever comes to me will never go
> hungry, and whoever believes in me
> will never be thirsty.
>
> For my Father's will is that everyone
> who looks to the Son and believes in him
> shall have eternal life, and I will raise
> them up at the last day.'
>
> John 6:35,40

Jesus spoke these words to the crowds, shortly after He fed more than five thousand hungry people with just five small loaves and two small fish.

The crowds hoped for more – and greater – material things from Jesus' miraculous powers but He had to disappoint them. His mission was not to satisfy their appetites for material pleasures and possessions but to meet their deep spiritual needs.

Jesus referred to Himself as the bread of life. He had come to earth to give life – eternal life. It was available to everyone who was hungry to know Jesus and to believe in Him. Today, Jesus still longs that people will have a hunger for Him.

Will you follow the crowds with their hunger for popularity, power, status, success, wealth and so much more; a hunger that will never truly be met?

Or will you choose to accept Jesus' invitation to follow Him? If you choose Jesus, your hunger will be satisfied and you will be safe with Him for eternity.

DEAR FATHER GOD

I know this to be true. I see this with my friends who have achieved and gained so much and yet are hungry for more. I do believe what Jesus has said. I am sure I shall only find real satisfaction in following Him. That is what I want to do.

AMEN

INSECURE?

The words of the Apostle:

> ... we who have fled to take hold of the hope
> set before us may be greatly encouraged.
> We have this hope as an anchor for the
> soul, firm and secure.

Hebrews 6:18b-19a

Water is an attraction for many people. Some enjoy a canal boat for the serenity and security it offers. For the adventurous, the exhilarating experience of white water rafting has greater appeal.

However, no white water enthusiast would want their life to resemble rafting, with the constant and desperate struggle to avoid overturning. Yet, some people's lives are a bit like that. They are continually battered by the roaring waters of life. They long to be secure in placid waters.

Even in the apparent safety of a harbour, a boat must be anchored; otherwise, it will gently drift away with the tide or be swept away in a storm.

In these verses, the writer uses the anchor as a symbol of the hope which keeps the Christian fully secure. It is as if the anchor is firmly embedded in an immovable rock. That rock is Jesus Himself.

Are you drifting or being battered? If so, why not anchor yourself to Jesus? With Him, you will be secure forever.

DEAR FATHER GOD

Dear Father God, I feel very insecure as I come up against one problem after another. I wonder how long I can manage to keep going. Please help me to know how I can have Jesus as a rock and how I can anchor my life to Him. Thank You.

AMEN

Rachael's* Story

"I emerged out of my childhood feeling lost, not really knowing my true identity and, most of all, needing to seek the love of others to heal my broken soul.

My mother suffered the awful disease of alcoholism and the depression which went with it. My whole world changed when I was just four years old, as my twin sister and I were taken away from our older sister, brother and father to a new home and stepfather. Life became very unpredictable for us: our mother would be aggressive when drunk and, at other times, vulnerable and suicidal. We lived in constant fear, experiencing a deep sense of rejection and despair.

A very happy memory from my childhood is the first occasion I heard about Jesus. I was about nine at the time and it was at a group run by a Christian man at school.

Then, about three years later some evangelists visited the area and encouraged children who were playing out on the streets to attend a mid- week service. What I heard taught from the Bible and the words of the songs we sang gave me hope. And I needed hope more than anything else. I still remember the line from one of the songs, "There will be no sorrow there, in my Father's house."

I am now a child of God, overwhelmed by His love and secure in His family.

Today, as a wife and as a mother of two daughters in their early teens, I have Jesus as my personal saviour. I no longer feel lost but now have a true identity in Jesus.

My favourite Bible verse is, "So if the Son sets you free, you will be free indeed."[1] For me, it was being set free from the long term effects of my dysfunctional childhood. I am now a child of God, overwhelmed by His love and secure in His family – a family which truly functions as God intends!

[1]John 8:36
*Not the real name of this person

45

INSULTED?

The crucifixion of Jesus:

Those who passed by hurled insults at him, shaking their heads and saying, 'So! You who are going to destroy the temple and build it in three days, come down from the cross and save yourself!'

Mark 15:29-30

Insults are hard to ignore. They wound us – as they are intended to - and we cannot pretend otherwise. They may remind us of something which we want to forget; perhaps something personal about us or our family; perhaps an unhappy episode from our past. Or they may just not be true.

Even as Jesus was dying on the cross, in great pain, the crowds hurled insults at Him. Their insults never had any element of truth: it was impossible to find fault in Him.

Their cruel and spiteful outbursts would have added to Jesus' anguish, just as insults hurt us. They also mocked Jesus by misquoting what He had said about the temple being destroyed and rebuilt in three days. They had not understood that Jesus was talking about His own body and how He would be raised to life again. And of course He was.

Instead of retaliating, Jesus entrusted Himself to Father God who judges justly.[1] When we are insulted, we should try to follow Jesus' example.

DEAR FATHER GOD

Those who insult me must hate me and I feel hatred towards them. I know I am wrong to have these feelings but it is hard to ignore remarks which are meant to hurt. Please help me not to retaliate and please protect my heart from insulting words.

AMEN

[1] 1 Peter 2:23

ISOLATED?

The words of King David:

> Where can I go from your Spirit?
> Where can I flee from your presence?

Psalm 139:7

The words of the Apostle Paul:

> For I am convinced that neither death
> nor life, neither angels nor demons,
> neither the present nor the future, nor any
> powers, neither height nor depth,
> nor anything else in all creation,
> will be able to separate us from the love
> of God that is in Christ Jesus our Lord.

Romans 8:38-39

It is only possible to know what it is like to be in prison if you have actually experienced it. Probably, the loss of freedom is the most difficult thing to cope with.

Prisoners must also find it immensely painful being separated from their family and friends and from their community. Some will have long periods of being isolated from other prisoners too. Of course, we can feel isolated even within our own homes.

The words of King David remind us that we are never separated from God. God is everywhere. Wherever we are, God is there. And the verses from the book of Romans are a reminder that God's love is always available to us; whatever our circumstances and however isolated we might find ourselves.

Are you isolated from family and friends? Or perhaps you have no family or, at least, no contact with them. Do not isolate yourself from God. Receive the love He offers you, right where you are.

DEAR FATHER GOD

I am isolated and it is very painful. I am thankful that nothing can separate me from Your love. Please help me to know that You are with me at all times and may the knowledge of Your presence and Your love keep me strong.

AMEN

LONELY?

Words of Jesus:

> 'I am the good shepherd; I know my
> sheep and my sheep know me...'

John 10:14

It is very painful when we have no one; when there is no one to ask how we are feeling; when there is no one who has the time or inclination to visit or call; when there is no one who realises how lonely we are.

Jesus likens Himself to a shepherd. Shepherds know and care for all their sheep. They care for each one individually. If one sheep goes off alone, the shepherd will go and search for it. The shepherd will never forget any one of his flock.

That is a wonderful illustration of how God sees us. We are all very precious to Him. He knows every one of us by name and we are never out of His sight, never alone. We may find that difficult to grasp but it is true.

Lonely? Then, entrust your life to Jesus, the good and perfect shepherd, and become one of His sheep. As one of His flock, you will be welcomed as a member of God's family. The steps you need to take are explained on pages 90-97.

DEAR FATHER GOD

I am beginning to realise just how lonely I am. It is very painful. It is staggering to think that You know every person on this earth by name – and that includes me. I do want Jesus to be my shepherd and I want to be part of Your family.

AMEN

LOST?

The words of a loving father:

> *"... But we had to celebrate and be glad,*
> *because this brother of yours was dead*
> *and is alive again; he was lost and is found."*

Luke 15:32

This verse comes at the end of the parable which Jesus told of The Prodigal (or Lost) Son.[1] In the story, the younger of two sons asks his father for his share of the inheritance and then leaves home.

The inheritance is soon squandered. Without any friends and barely able to get enough food to survive, he is lost to know what to do.

Eventually, his thoughts turn to home. Reluctantly (and ashamed), he decides to return, just hoping that his father might show mercy. All he wants is to be hired as a servant.

He need not have feared. His father is so thrilled when he sees his son in the distance that he runs to meet him and embraces him. The father then lays on a feast to celebrate the lost son's return.

That is a wonderful picture of God, our Heavenly Father, who longs to welcome back all who recognise that they are lost. Are you?

DEAR FATHER GOD

I am like that lost son. There was a time when I really did love You. Then I drifted away, thinking I did not need You. How wrong I was. I am very sorry. Please accept me back.

AMEN

[1] Luke 15:11

WILL'S STORY

"I have a very loving family and, looking back, I wonder why I began taking drugs as a 13-year old, except for the fact that my friends and I simply wanted to experience them. As I continued, all my relationships suffered and I isolated myself from my family.

It was almost inevitable that I would move on to harder drugs and it was almost inevitable that the more I filled myself with drugs the emptier I would feel inside. I experienced an overwhelming and terrifying feeling of worthlessness. I could not believe that anyone could love me.

Finally – after more than ten years – I reached the point of knowing that I had a decision to make; to stick with my life of despair and emptiness, enslaved to drugs or to look for a life of purpose and rebuild relationships. I suppose I was a bit like the 'prodigal son'.[1] Like him, I was ready to go back and look for love and acceptance.

I know now that God was reaching out to me, opening my eyes to see the mess I was in and lifting me from my pit of despair. I know that it was God who led me to go to church. And I know that it was God who spoke to me during an Alpha Course, telling me how much He loved me and how Jesus had died for me. I said sorry to God for rebelling against Him and I asked Jesus to come into my empty life.

... NOW I KNOW THAT I AM NOT WORTHLESS: JESUS PAID SUCH A BIG PRICE FOR MY REBELLION AGAINST GOD.

For the next few months I felt physically light as if I was floating around! What a contrast that was to the heaviness and darkness of my old life. It took a long time to sink in. But now I know that I am *not* worthless: Jesus paid such a big price for my rebellion against God.

*Not the real name of this person
[1]See page 52

MALIGNED?

Words of King David:

> **Do not let those gloat over me**
> **who are my enemies without cause;**
> **do not let those who hate me without reason**
> **maliciously wink the eye.**
>
> **They do not speak peaceably,**
> **but devise false accusations**
> **against those who live quietly in the land.**
>
> Psalm 35:19-20

"Sticks and stones may break my bones but words will never hurt me." This saying aims to encourage children to ignore what others say about them but, as a statement, it is simply untrue. Malicious words can be more destructive than sticks and stones. And if the words are untrue, then the pain becomes even more difficult to bear.

When enemies of King David made false accusations against him, he asked God to intervene and to put them to shame. The

Bible says that we should not take revenge but allow God to act: "'It is mine to avenge; I will repay,' says the Lord." [1]

When false accusations were made against Jesus, resulting in His death, He did not defend Himself. Instead, as He hung on the cross, He asked God to forgive those responsible.

If you have been maligned, try not to respond with anger. That will only add to your pain. Why not ask God to help you follow Jesus' example?

DEAR FATHER GOD

You know that the things being said about me are untrue and they are really hurting me. Please cause these people to stop. And please help me to put aside my anger and forgive them.

AMEN

[1]Romans 12:19

OPPRESSED?

Words of the Psalmist:

> He upholds the cause of the oppressed
> and gives food to the hungry.
> The LORD sets prisoners free,
> the LORD gives sight to the blind,
> the LORD lifts up those
> who are bowed down,
> the LORD loves the righteous.

Psalm 146:7-8

These verses remind us that God is compassionate: He has a concern for everyone in need but especially for those whom society looks down upon. Amongst others, the Psalmist mentions the oppressed, that is the downtrodden; the exploited; the disadvantaged; and the underprivileged.

Jesus demonstrated the reality of God's compassion when He was on earth. He always had time for people who were oppressed by others. That compassion was seen in many of the healings He performed; of lepers; of the lame; of the demon-possessed.

It was also seen in His choice of 'friends': He became known as a 'friend of tax collectors and sinners'. (Tax collectors were resented by their fellow Jews because they worked for the Romans and were corrupt in charging extra tax for their own pockets.)

If you are oppressed, there can be no better friend to have than Jesus. He knows just how you are feeling. He has time for you if you will take time to speak with Him.

DEAR FATHER GOD

I take great comfort when I read of the sort of people Jesus chose to spend time with. I think He would have spent time with me. Please help me to understand how I can get to know Jesus as a friend.

AMEN

OVERWHELMED?

Words of Jesus:

'Therefore everyone who hears these words of mine and puts them into practice is like a wise man who built his house on the rock...'

Matthew 7:24

Jesus spoke of two builders: one who built his house upon foundations of rock and the other who simply built his house upon sand. It was inevitable that the house without foundations would collapse when a severe thunderstorm came. And that is what happened.

Jesus used this to illustrate the importance of building our lives upon a proper foundation, in order that we should not be overwhelmed by the pressures, tensions and struggles which can be a part of everyday life.

The truly wise man is the one who puts his trust in Jesus. He knows that Jesus will be there to help him when there is a danger of being overwhelmed by troubles. The wise man's faith becomes the very foundation of his life.

God Himself has declared, 'No, there is no other Rock; I know not one.'[1] If you are being swamped by problems which threaten to overwhelm you, why not start building your life on Jesus, with Him right at the centre?

DEAR FATHER GOD

I am so vulnerable because I panic when I think I am going to be overwhelmed by a crisis. I need something or someone I can really trust. I will ask Jesus to be my rock: I believe that only He can be the rock I need.

AMEN

[1]Isaiah 44:8

REJECTED?

The trial of Jesus:

> But the whole crowd shouted, 'Away
> with this man! Release Barabbas to us!'
> (Barabbas had been thrown into prison for
> an insurrection in the city, and for murder.)
> Wanting to release Jesus, Pilate appealed
> to them again. But they kept shouting,
> 'Crucify him! Crucify him!'

Luke 23:18-21

Rejection is always hard to accept, for we all have a fundamental need 'to belong' and 'to be wanted'. It is hard when your friends – even your family - turn their back on you; when your job applications are continually rejected and when you are told by a charity that you are 'not suitable' to be a volunteer.

Jesus knows all about rejection. Pontius Pilate, the Roman governor, wanted to release Jesus (under the custom of releasing a prisoner at the annual Passover festival). But the crowd rejected Jesus in favour of Barabbas who was being held in prison for insurrection and murder.

As Barabbas was freed, so Jesus was condemned to be crucified. How did He feel as people who once followed Him sided with the religious leaders in rejecting Him?

We know that Father God will never reject anyone who turns to Him, believing on Jesus. So, if you believe on Jesus you need never fear God's rejection.

DEAR FATHER GOD

Thank You that I can come to You and will never be rejected. Please help me to overcome the pain from all the rejection I have experienced. And please help me to follow Jesus' example in not retaliating against those who have hurt me.

AMEN

RESTLESS?

Words of the Apostle Paul:

But now in Christ Jesus you who once were far away have been brought near by the blood of Christ. For he himself is our peace, ...

Ephesians 2:13-14a

Let the peace of Christ rule in your hearts, ...

Colossians 3:15a

The most successful of people often seem to be the most restless. For many, the taste of success – however they might measure it – only gives them a longing for more. That is true in all areas of life.

Of course, ambition is not wrong: it is good to have goals which stretch us. At the same time, there is a danger of being constantly restless; never satisfied; always wanting something more (or just something different).

But striving after more is not the biggest cause of restlessness. The main reason for being restless is failing to understand the real purpose of life. We were created in God's image in order to be in relationship with Him and to please Him. Unless that becomes our purpose, we will always be restless.

If you want to be free from constant restlessness, pursue God's purpose for your life by trusting His Son, Jesus Christ. Allow Him to rule in your heart and to be your peace.

DEAR FATHER GOD

I have been restless for as long as I can remember. But that is not how I want my life to be. I want to be settled and satisfied and to have peace in my heart. I realise I need Jesus in my heart.

AMEN

Anna's* Story

"As a child, I don't think I ever doubted that God made the universe but I never really thought that we could actually engage with Him.

As a teenager, my rebellion was fairly mild in comparison with others. In my 20s I enjoyed a good social life but nothing extreme. However, I was always restless. If I wasn't happy in a job, I left. If I wasn't happy in a relationship, I left. If I wasn't happy where I was living, I moved. I was in control. I was my own boss. I was in charge of making myself happy. It always seemed to work ... for a while!

Two years ago I came into contact with a church through a mums' and toddlers' group. At the time, I was thinking about a broken relationship in my life. Unusually for me, I hadn't been able to 'fix' it.

I joined a small Bible study group. During a study of Jesus speaking with the 'woman at the well'[1], I had an overwhelming sense that Jesus was speaking to me (although my life bore no resemblance to hers). I felt a massive sense of safety as I invited Jesus into my life.

I am a changed person.
I am no longer restless and
in Jesus I am safe forever.

A few months later, at a time when I was feeling rather overwhelmed and quite low, I was reading the Bible[2] with a friend and it became so clear that I really did love Jesus. It was a huge moment of realisation. Never again would I need to run from a difficult feeling or situation. I knew that I could stand firm in the armour of God!

I am a changed person. I am no longer restless and in Jesus I am safe forever. And I now know that I don't have to fix everything!

[1] See page 16
[2] Ephesians 6:10-18 (The Armour of God)
*Not the real name of this person

SCARED?

Words of King David:

> Truly he is my rock and my salvation;
> he is my fortress, I shall not be shaken.
> My salvation and my honour depend on God;
> he is my mighty rock, my refuge.
> Trust in him at all times, you people;
> pour out your hearts to him,
> for God is our refuge.

Psalm 62: 6-8

David's early life as a shepherd boy may have been fairly peaceful. He did not seem to be unduly troubled by the danger of prowling lions and wolves. Nor was he unduly troubled by the threat from Goliath, the great Philistine giant whom he then defeated.

Later, however, David did receive some death threats which caused him to be scared. First, King Saul tried to kill him when he became jealous of David's popularity with the people. After that, David was forced to escape from his own son, Absalom.

When we read some of David's Psalms, we see that he often cried out to God to ask for protection from his enemies. And he was able to say that God was his rock, his fortress and his refuge. God never failed him.

Whatever your circumstances, that can also be true for you. God can be your rock and your refuge.

DEAR FATHER GOD

If you know everything, then You will know the situation I am in right now and I am scared. I am willing to admit it. Please protect me. I want You to be my refuge just as You were King David's refuge.

AMEN

SINKING?

Words of King David:

> I waited patiently for the LORD;
> he turned to me and heard my cry.
> He lifted me out of the slimy pit,
> out of the mud and mire;
> he set my feet on a rock and
> gave me a firm place to stand.
> He put a new song in my mouth,
> a hymn of praise to our God.
>
> Psalm 40:1-3a

David begins this Psalm by describing God's help like being rescued from a slimy pit. It is a picture of David being utterly helpless, sinking slowly into the slimy mud.

Later in the Psalm, David makes a further urgent plea to God to save him, 'Be pleased to save me, LORD; come quickly, LORD, to help me.' (v13). He is overwhelmed by further troubles which, he says, are 'too many to count'. Some of them are the result of his own sin.

After pleading for God's mercy, David finally prays this prayer (v17):

> 'But as for me, I am poor and needy;
> may the LORD think of me.
> You are my help and my deliverer;
> you are my God, do not delay.'

God is still lifting people out of their 'slimy pits' when they recognise how helpless they are and decide to cry out to Him. If you identify with David's circumstances   with problems too many to count – why not cry out to God as David did?

DEAR FATHER GOD

With all the issues I am facing, I feel as though I am sinking in a slimy pit, like David imagined he was. Please hear my cry for help and deliver me. I want to be on firm ground and able to praise You.

AMEN

TROUBLED?

Words of Jesus to His disciples:

'Peace I leave with you; my peace I give you.
I do not give to you as the world gives.
Do not let your hearts be troubled and
do not be afraid. ...'

John 14:27

Jesus spoke these words to comfort His disciples. After sharing 'The Last Supper' together, Jesus had explained that He would shortly be leaving them. This was devastating news. Naturally, they were troubled about what would happen to them: they had spent the last three years with Jesus, having given up everything to follow Him.

Jesus assured the disciples that He would not leave them on their own like orphans: God the Father would send the Holy Spirit to be their Helper.[1] And because of His presence in their hearts, the disciples would enjoy peace.

That promise was not just for those disciples. Today, every believer on the Lord Jesus Christ has His Holy Spirit living in them. They, too, can enjoy perfect peace in times of trouble.

That does not mean that followers of Jesus do not experience trouble, for we live in a troubled world. What it does mean is that, despite their troubles, God's peace will guard their hearts and minds.[2]

DEAR FATHER GOD

More than anything else, I want to have peace in my heart, despite everything that is going on in my life. Please give me peace that I may be able to cope with the troubles I have to deal with.

AMEN

[1] John 14:16,18   [2] Philippians 4:7

UNLOVED?

The Apostle John wrote:

See what great love the Father has lavished on us, that we should be called children of God! And that is what we are!

1 John 3:1a

Whoever does not love does not know God, because God is love. This is how God showed his love among us: he sent his one and only Son into the world that we might live through him.

1 John 4:8-9

To love and to be loved are two of the most basic needs of human beings. We often take them for granted.

Sadly, because of broken relationships and broken families, many people do not have those needs met. Some may never have truly experienced love at all.

The Bible tells us that God is love. He loves us far more than we can possibly imagine and He wants every one of us to be a true child of His.

These are not just nice words to make us feel good. God proved His love by providing the way by which we can be rescued. He did that by sending Jesus to die for us.

Have you experienced God's love for yourself? If not, why not consider inviting Him to take control of your life and so become a part of His family? The steps you need to take to do that are explained on pages 90-97.

DEAR FATHER GOD

I do feel unloved. For years I have longed to find love and to be able to show love to others but I have never succeeded. Please help me to understand how I can truly know You as a father, to be Your child and receive Your love.

AMEN

UNWORTHY?

Words of the younger son in the story of The Lost Son:

> " ... I will set out and go back to my father
> and say to him: Father, I have sinned
> against heaven and against you. I am
> no longer worthy to be called your son;
> make me like one of your hired servants."

Luke 15:18-19

In Jesus' story of The Lost (or Prodigal) Son, the younger son decided that he had had enough of his job of feeding pigs. That was how low he had sunk, having wasted his share of his father's inheritance.

He thought that the best he could hope for was to get his dad to take him on as one of his servants: he no longer felt worthy of being his son. But he need not have worried: his father was so relieved and delighted to see his son again. (See 'Lost?', page 52)

Being unworthy is not a barrier to being accepted by God. The truth is we are all unworthy. None of us deserve God's love and acceptance, whether we have really 'messed up' or whether we can boast about our 'good works'.

The wonderful news is that Father God counts us worthy when we come to Him in the name of His Son, Jesus Christ. Jesus is the only One who is worthy.

DEAR FATHER GOD

I am so grateful that I do not have to pass any test to show that I am worthy to be Your child. I know I would fail every test. Thank You for counting me worthy and for accepting me because I come to You in the name of Jesus.

AMEN

Amanda's*
Story

At some stage, most churchgoing parents will find themselves having to coerce a reluctant child to attend church with them. For me, it was a question of being 'dragged along' to church by my seven-year-old daughter. I am so thankful that I was!

As a child, my home life was comfortable but ill-health and bullying at school left me feeling rejected and worthless. Then at 21, I suffered severe depression due to further ill-health.

I concluded that I was simply not worthy of being loved.

I was thankful for a period of improved health and was eager to be loved and have a sense of belonging. In my search for this, I gave myself over to a series of less than loving relationships. The result was almost inevitable; more rejection and a greater sense of worthlessness.

Then at 26, I met my husband and when our son was two years old, I fell pregnant with our daughter. However, five months into the pregnancy, my husband started to abuse me; physically and emotionally. Within two years, I was a single mum and, again, I felt rejected. I concluded that I was simply not worthy of being loved.

It was five years later when my daughter astounded me with her announcement, "Mummy, I've decided I'd like to be a Christian". A reluctant mother escorted her daughter to church.

As the minister began to preach, I was filled with an amazing sense of having come home. I did not know anyone in the congregation and, yet, I was certain that I was exactly where I belonged. Although nobody touched me, I felt the embrace of God's love.

I have found all that I need in God's love for me …

I have found all that I need in God's love for me, through Jesus Christ. That is one relationship which has lasted: I know it will last forever.

*Not the real name of this person

WEAK?

Words concerning Jesus:

For we do not have a high priest who is unable to feel sympathy for our weaknesses, but we have one who has been tempted in every way, just as we are – yet he did not sin. Let us then approach God's throne of grace with confidence, so that we may receive mercy and find grace to help us in our time of need.

Hebrews 4:15-16

We may think that God is far too remote in heaven to be able to understand the realities of life on earth; the struggles which wear us down, leaving us so weak.

But that is not true. God knows everything about every one of us and cares about each of us personally. Also, these verses remind us that we come to God through Jesus (who acts as a high priest) and Jesus is certainly able to sympathise with our weakness.

Jesus came to earth as a human being and experienced the difficulties and temptations of daily living just as we do. He had enemies who despised Him: they were always looking to find fault with Him. In His weakness, Jesus constantly sought help from His Father in heaven.

If you are feeling weak, do not hold back from asking God for His help. You can approach Him with confidence, knowing that He is aware of your circumstances and that He wants to show you His grace and kindness.

DEAR FATHER GOD

I am feeling weak and finding it difficult to cope with everything that is expected of me. I usually try to struggle on in my own strength but I cannot do that anymore. You know what I need to do. Please help me. Thank You.

AMEN

WEARY?

An invitation from Jesus:

> 'Come to me, all you who are weary and
> burdened, and I will give you rest.
> Take my yoke upon you and learn from me,
> for I am gentle and humble in heart, and
> you will find rest for your souls. For my
> yoke is easy and my burden is light.'
>
> Matthew 11:28-30

Jesus always had a special concern for those who were weary with the strains and stresses of life. They were the people who really wanted to hear what Jesus had to say and how He could meet their needs.

The attitude of the religious leaders was quite different. As well as being self-righteous, they considered themselves self-sufficient. Their pride would not allow them to accept they had a need of anything or anyone. Certainly they would never admit that there was anything they could learn or gain from spending time with Jesus.

So, this invitation was for the ordinary people of the day. It was for those who recognised that life did get tough at times and who were willing to admit to being weary and burdened.

Jesus' invitation has not expired: it remains open today. Are you weary with family or work responsibilities – or both? If so, is there anything to prevent you from asking Jesus to give you rest as He has promised?

DEAR FATHER GOD

I am not too proud to admit to being weary. Every morning, I realise that I will never manage to do everything that people expect of me. Please help me not to take on more than I need to. And please help me to find rest for my soul with You.

AMEN

WORRIED?

Words of Jesus:

Then Jesus said to his disciples: 'Therefore I tell you, do not worry about your life, what you will eat; or about your body, what you will wear. For life is more than food, and the body more than clothes.

Who of you by worrying can add a single hour to your life? Since you cannot do this very little thing, why do you worry about the rest? ...'

Luke 12:22-23, 25-26

Often, it is uncertainty about the future that causes us to worry: and worry is like a thief who robs us of our peace of mind.

Jesus had just told a story of a rich farmer who was obsessed with safeguarding his future. Jesus called him a fool, because life itself is uncertain. He would soon die and all his labours would be wasted. It is foolish to plan for the future but leave God out of your life.

Jesus then told His disciples not to worry: worrying does not achieve anything. He reminds them that we are far more valuable to God than the birds and God feeds them.

Jesus assured the disciples that God knew all about their needs and they should leave the future in His hands. Instead of worrying, they were to focus on seeking God's kingdom.

Are you worrying about what might happen? It can be hard not to - but read again those words of Jesus. Try to follow His advice and trust Him.

DEAR FATHER GOD

I often worry about the future. Please help me to hand my worries over to You and to be able to trust You to provide for my needs. I realise that You know everything about me and my situation. Thank You for caring for me.

AMEN

WORTHLESS?

Jesus and the blind beggar:

> He called out, 'Jesus, Son of David,
> have mercy on me!'
> Those who led the way rebuked him
> and told him to be quiet, but he shouted
> all the more, 'Son of David, have mercy
> on me!' Jesus stopped and ordered
> the man to be brought to him.
>
> Luke 18:38-40a

The blind beggar's cries for mercy were an embarrassment to the people. They must have thought a beggar was not someone worth bothering Jesus with. But they were wrong. They should have known that Jesus always had compassion on those in need.

Some of the people may have felt sorry for him but it seems that most of them looked down at him. Many might have considered him a worthless member of society. Perhaps that is how he thought about himself - worthless.

Jesus saw him quite differently: a very precious man created in God's own image. Jesus never ignored a cry for mercy and that is still the case today, for the Bible tells us that He is "the same yesterday and today and for ever."[1]

If you feel worthless for whatever reason, call out to Jesus. He will not ignore your cry. Your circumstances are not important to Him. What matters to Him is your desire to love Him and to follow Him.

DEAR FATHER GOD

I am sure that people look upon me as being worthless. That is how I think of myself. Please God, have mercy on me just as Jesus showed mercy to that beggar and please help me through this difficult time.

AMEN

[1] Hebrews 13:8

OUR BIGGEST STRUGGLE

OUR BIGGEST STRUGGLE

There is one struggle which is always in the background. Yet we may not even recognise it as a struggle. It is the struggle to obey God's laws.

The Apostle Paul summed it up very well:

> **For I do not do the good I want to do, but the evil I do not want to do – this I keep on doing. Now if I do what I do not want to do, it is no longer I who do it, but it is sin living in me that does it.**

Romans 7:19-20

Paul wanted to do the right things but was always failing. He knew the reason: the sinful nature within him.

Paul really struggled with these bad inner pressures. However, many people never think about this personal struggle between right and wrong. We tend only to think about the struggles which cause us pain. But, when it comes to our problem with sin – breaking God's law - we must consider the pain we cause Him.

Why is God hurt when we sin?

When God created the world He made us in His likeness, so that we might relate with Him and live to glorify Him. But that has become impossible because of our sinful nature (which we inherited from Adam and Eve when they disobeyed God in the Garden of Eden).

The Bible tells us: **"… for all have sinned and fall short of the glory of God."** Romans 3:23

God is absolutely holy and pure. He cannot tolerate sin and that is a barrier between God and us.

If God hates sin, does that mean He is not a God of love?

As God is just, He cannot simply ignore our sin. There has to be a punishment for it.

> The Bible tells us: **For the wages of sin is death...** Romans 6:23a

However, He is certainly loving and merciful. His love is so great that He longs to restore us rather than punish us. He made that possible by sending His Son, Jesus, to come to earth as a human being and to die in our place.

> The Bible tells us: **But God demonstrates his own love for us in this: while we were still sinners, Christ died for us.** Romans 5:8

Does that mean God will not punish us?

It means that we will not have to face God's punishment *but only if we choose to receive God's forgiveness*. We can ask God to forgive us if we believe that Jesus Christ paid the penalty for our sins and if we are willing to allow Jesus to rule our lives.

Receiving the forgiveness of sins is described in the Bible as being 'born again'.[1] It is the start of a new life as a follower of Jesus.

What happens if we decide not to accept Jesus?

If we say, 'No', to God's rescue plan, we will be punished ourselves. That will happen when Jesus returns to earth, for He will come to judge – and punish – everyone who has not accepted God's offer of forgiveness.

It will be the most awful punishment of being separated from God forever.

The Bible tells us: **... Whoever believes in him is not condemned, but whoever does not believe stands condemned already because they have not believed in the name of God's one and only Son.** John 3:18

[1]John 3:1-21

JESUS

Why was Jesus, the Son of God,

BETRAYED,
ABANDONED,
FALSELY ACCUSED,
MALIGNED,
CONDEMNED,
FLOGGED,
MOCKED,
SPAT ON,
ASSAULTED,
INSULTED,
RIDICULED,
HUMILIATED

– and hung on a cross to die?

Anyone unfamiliar with the story might assume that Jesus had been responsible for the most horrendous crimes – perhaps war crimes, acts of terrorism or serial killings – to deserve to be treated as He was and then be put to death.

His brutal crucifixion, at the age of about 33, was certainly the greatest miscarriage of justice in history but it did not destroy God's plan: it fulfilled it.

Jesus' purpose for coming to earth was to die - in our place. He willingly took the punishment which we all deserve; from the worst of criminals to the most 'upright' of law-abiding citizens.

He did that so that all our sins might be forgiven.

What do I need to do to become a Christian?

You can become a follower of Jesus and have all your sins forgiven by:

- **accepting** that you have not kept God's laws and deserve to be punished,

- **believing** that only Jesus can rescue you from God's punishment,

- **confessing** the wrong things in your life and repenting of them, that is, turning away from them,

- **deciding** to live to please God as a follower of Jesus.

If you are ready to take those steps, you can do so now by using the following prayer.

DEAR FATHER GOD

I am very sorry for everything in my life, past and present, which is not right. I now repent of my sin.

Thank You for sending Jesus to die in my place, for my sins, in order to save me from the punishment which I deserve.

I want to live to please Jesus and to make Him the centre of my life - to be my King.

Please forgive all my sins and accept me as Your child. Please fill me with Your Holy Spirit to help me live a new life.

AMEN

If you have been sincere with this prayer, God has received you as His child. All your sins – past, present and future – are forgiven.

And what now? You will need to grow as a Christian and that can only happen if you meet regularly with other Christians where the Bible is taught carefully. Therefore, the first step is to link with a local church and with Christians who will be able to help and support you.

BeaconLight

You may find these other resources from BeaconLight helpful

www.wordatwork.org.uk

A free, unique, expository devotional email which allows the Bible to energise your working day. It is read by over 30,000 people in 198 countries.

CrossCheck
www.crosscheck.org.uk

A straightforward and engaging way to learn how to explain the gospel clearly and lead people to Christ without fudging or forcing.

This explores the freedom which we can experience when we forgive others – and the even greater freedom and joy when we know God's forgiveness.

A straightforward Biblical response to that very question, 'Can I forgive myself?' It explains the need we all have of God's forgiveness and how we can receive it.

A workbook of 16 essential Bible studies to help you unlock the truth of God's Word.

150 High Street Banstead Surrey SM7 2NZ
Email: books@beaconlight.co.uk Phone: 01737 357103